Xin Chào,
VIETNAM

by Meghan Gottschall

CHERRY LAKE PUBLISHING · ANN ARBOR, MICHIGAN

CHERRY LAKE PRESS

Published in the United States of America by Cherry Lake Publishing Group
Ann Arbor, Michigan
www.cherrylakepublishing.com

Reading Adviser: Marla Conn, MS, Ed., Literacy specialist, Read-Ability, Inc.

Photo Credits: ©Juanmonino/iStock/Getty Images, cover (map), ©wiratgasem/Moment/Getty Images, cover (bottom), ©jack0m/DigitalVision Vectors/Getty Images, cover (globe), ©filo/DigitalVision Vectors/Getty Images, cover (background), ©Ho Ngoc Binh/Moment/Getty Images, 1, ©Maurice Koop/Flickr, 3, ©Jakkree Thampitakkull/Moment/Getty Images, 4, ©Nitat Termmee/Moment/Getty Images, 5, ©MuchMania/iStock/Getty Images, 6, ©ErmakovaElena/iStock/Getty Images, 7, ©ExploringMekong.com/Moment/Getty Images, 8, ©Truong Phuong Tram/Moment/Getty Images, 9 (top), ©Photographer/Moment/Getty Images, 9 (bottom), ©jacus/iStock/Getty Images, 10, ©Stocktrek Images/Getty Images, 11, ©Rapeepong Puttakumwong/Moment/Getty Images, 12, ©raclro/E+/Getty Images, 13, ©nevarpp/iStock Editorial/Getty Images, 14, ©duybox/iStock Editorial/Getty Images, 15, ©MeogiaPhoto/Moment/Getty Images, 16 (top), ©USAID Vietnam/Wikimedia, 16 (bottom), ©Martin H. Simon-Pool/Getty Images, 18, ©Rhombur/iStock Editorial/Getty Images, 20, ©shaadjutt/iStock/Getty Images, 21 (top), ©Ho Ngoc Binh/Moment/Getty Images, 21 (bottom), ©NicolasMcComber/E+/Getty Images, 22, ©hoangtran7ice/iStock/Getty Images, 23, ©Yavuz Sriyildiz/Moment Unreleased/Getty Images, 24, ©Richard Nyberg/Planet Pix via ZUMA Wire/Newscom, 25, ©Phung Huynh Vu Qui/Moment/Getty Images, 26, ©John Seaton Callahan/Moment/Getty Images, 27, ©Pham Ty/Moment/Getty Images, 28, ©Mint Images RF/Getty Images, 29, ©vinhdav/iStock Editorial/Getty Images, 30, ©Rike_/iStock/Getty Images, 32, ©Wilfried Krecichwost/Photodisc/Getty Images, 33, ©cuongvnd/Moment/Getty Images, 34, ©Thang Tat Nguyen/Moment/Getty Images, 35, ©xuanhuongho/iStock Editorial/Getty Images, 36, ©hadynyah/E+/Getty Images, 38, ©hadynyah/Getty Images, 39, ©Thanh Thuy/Moment/Getty Images, 40 (top), ©Foxys_forest_manufacture/iStock/Getty Images, 40 (bottom), ©Walter Bibikow/Stone/Getty Images, 41, ©Creativeye99/iStock/Getty Images, 42, ©intek1/iStock/Getty Images, 43, ©manuel cazzaniga/Moment/Getty Images, 44, ©bhofack2/iStock/Getty Images, 45

Library of Congress Cataloging-in-Publication Data has been filed and is available at catalog.loc.gov

Cherry Lake Publishing Group would like to acknowledge the work of the Partnership for 21st Century Learning, a Network of Battelle for Kids. Please visit http://www.battelleforkids.org/networks/p21 for more information.

Printed in the United States of America
Corporate Graphics

TABLE OF CONTENTS

CHAPTER 1

WELCOME TO VIETNAM!

Rice terraces cover the hills of Northeast Vietnam.

The country of Vietnam has a history stretching back around 5,000 years. The land is full of mountains, jungles, and beaches. Ancient temples and towns can be found in the countryside. There are also busy, modern cities. People zoom around on motorbikes. Over time, the nation's culture has been influenced by different groups. The Chinese and French have both controlled Vietnam at different times. The country's **communist** government has also left its mark.

Vietnam is located in Southeast Asia. Laos and Cambodia lie to the west, with China to the north. The Gulf of Thailand, the Gulf of Tonkin, and the South China Sea form Vietnam's water borders. There are more than 2,000 miles (3,219 kilometers) of coastline.

The bar-bellied pitta is only found in Vietnam, Cambodia, Laos, and Thailand.

ACTIVITY

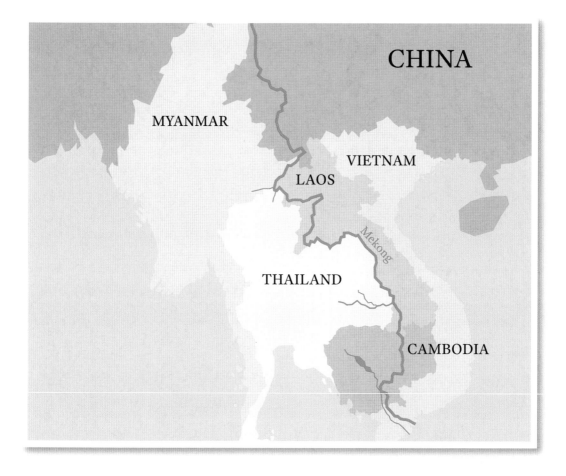

Rivers naturally flow downhill, from high areas to low areas, until they eventually flow into the ocean. Many rivers start in one country and end in another. Place a piece of paper over the map above and trace the route of the Mekong River. Find its start in China. Then follow its route through Laos, Cambodia, and Vietnam until you reach the ocean. Look up the cities, towns, and other sites of interest that are next to the river. Are there many towns along the Mekong? Why do you think people first settled along rivers?

Vietnam is long and skinny. At its narrowest point, the country is just 30 miles (48 km) wide. The total area is about 127,000 square miles (328,928 square km). This is about the size of the state of New Mexico.

Vietnam is divided into eight geographical regions. The northern half is divided into the Northeast, the Northwest, the Red River **Delta**, and the North Central Coast. The southern half is made up of the South Central Coast, the Central Highlands, the Southeast, and the Mekong River Delta.

It takes 1 to 3 days of hiking to reach the summit of Fansipan Mountain. A cable car makes the almost 4-mile (6.4 km) trip in 15 minutes.

The northern regions have mountains, hills, and plains. Hanoi, the capital, is situated there. The Red River winds its way through. Fansipan, the highest peak in the country, is in the north.

The Dãy Trường Sơn, or Annamite mountain range, runs down the western side of the central part. Beaches and harbors mark the eastern coastline.

The Mekong River flows through the south. The land around this wide delta is rich for farming. Ho Chi Minh City, the country's largest city, is found in the south.

The lotus is Vietnam's national flower. At night, the flower closes and sinks below the water.

The Ben Thanh Market is one of the oldest sites in Ho Chi Minh City.

Water Buffalo

Water buffalo are often considered Vietnam's national animal. Wild ones can be 7 feet (2 meters) tall and can weigh up to 2,650 pounds (1,202 kilograms). Others have been domesticated. They are smaller and are used as work animals. Farmers use them to plow rice paddies.

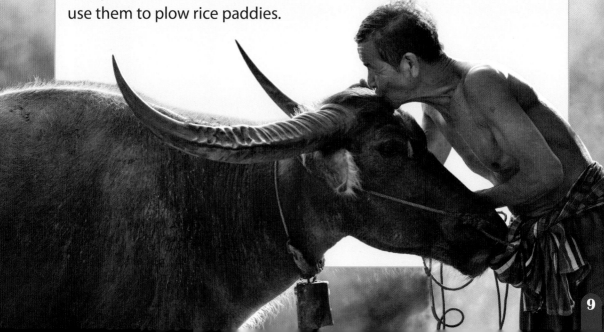

Most of Vietnam has a tropical climate. It is typically hot and wet, with two seasons: rainy and dry. May to October is the rainy season. Heavy **monsoon** rains fall almost every day during this time. Roads can flood quickly and make it difficult to get around.

In the tropical center and south, there is little temperature variation. The temperature is often around 90 degrees Fahrenheit (32 degrees Celsius) year-round, but it can range from 70 to 90°F (21 to 32°C).

There is more temperature variation in the north, which is in a temperate zone. Summers in the north are still hot, humid, and wet. Winters are cool and dry. Temperatures range from 50 to 90°F (10 to 32°C).

Water Pollution

Water pollution is a growing problem in Vietnam. The country's industries and cities have grown quickly. This has created lots of pollution from untreated sewage and industrial waste in the nation's rivers and oceans. Many beaches are also covered in plastic waste. Work is being done to teach people about the dangers of this kind of pollution.

Tropical storms occur during the summer months. Swirling winds and thunderstorms form over water. When they hit land, they can cause damage and injuries. If winds reach more than 74 miles (119 km) per hour, the storm is known as a **typhoon**.

In 2013, Typhoon Haiyan ripped roofs off of houses and uprooted trees in northern Vietnam.

In Vietnam, douc monkeys climb trees in the central and northern jungles. Tonkin snub-nosed monkeys make their homes in the northern mountains. Giant lizards called Asian water monitors live near the water. They have also been found in cities. In 2019, researchers filmed a rabbit-sized animal called a silver-backed chevrotain. Sometimes it is called a Vietnamese mouse deer. Scientists had thought they were extinct.

Chevrotains are the smallest hooved animals. They stand around 12 inches (30 centimeters) tall.

CHAPTER 2

BUSINESS AND GOVERNMENT IN VIETNAM

After World War II ended in 1945, France took control over southern Vietnam. North Vietnam declared itself an independent country. Fighting broke out between the communist government in the north and anti-communist forces in the south. The war lasted until 1975. The north won and took control over the south. This created the Republic of Vietnam.

U.S. Involvement in the Vietnam War

What the United States calls the Vietnam War (1955–1975) is known as "the American War" in Vietnam. The United States joined the fight in 1965. They sided with southern Vietnamese forces who didn't want the country to be under communist rule. U.S. troops left in 1973. Around 60,000 U.S. soldiers died during the conflict.

Today, under communist rule, the state still owns many businesses. However, private companies are beginning to own more of them. This has helped the economy grow.

People are employed in many ways in Vietnam. Around 39 percent work in agriculture. Around 35 percent have service jobs, many of them in cities. Around 26 percent work in industry, such as in **textile** factories.

More than 2.5 million people work in Vietnam's textile industry. This is around the same as the population of Chicago.

Rice is the most important crop in Vietnam. Rice paddies are found in the Mekong and Red River Deltas. In the mountains, farmers grow tea and coffee.

Farming is hard work. A lot of planting is still done by hand. Droughts have caused some workers to abandon farming. They move to urban areas to find work.

The seafood industry also provides many jobs. Vietnam is a major **exporter** of shrimp.

Most of Vietnam's shrimp is exported to other countries in Europe and Asia.

One of Vietnam's major exports is clothing and shoes. The country is the world's fourth-largest clothing exporter. Working conditions in factories are difficult. People work long hours to make enough money to live on. Minimum wage has increased, but many people still struggle to pay for basic needs like food and housing. Many factory workers make $125 to $180 a month.

Many houses in Hanoi's Old Quarter were built during the time of French colonial rule in the 1800s.

To support the textile industry, Vietnam imports raw materials. Rubber products are brought in to make shoes. Different fabrics are imported to make all kinds of clothing. Machines to make these products also come from other countries.

Đặng Thị Ngọc Thịnh

Đặng Thị Ngọc Thịnh was the first female president of Vietnam. She served for one month in 2018 after having been elected vice president. Thịnh took over the office after the president died and held it until the next president was elected. Recently, many women have been elected to the office of vice president.

2017 TRADING PARTNERS

Vietnam has many important trading partners. Trading partners are the countries where Vietnam sends its exports or where its imports come from. Here is a graph showing Vietnam's top import and export partners as of 2017. Many of these are nearby countries in Asia.

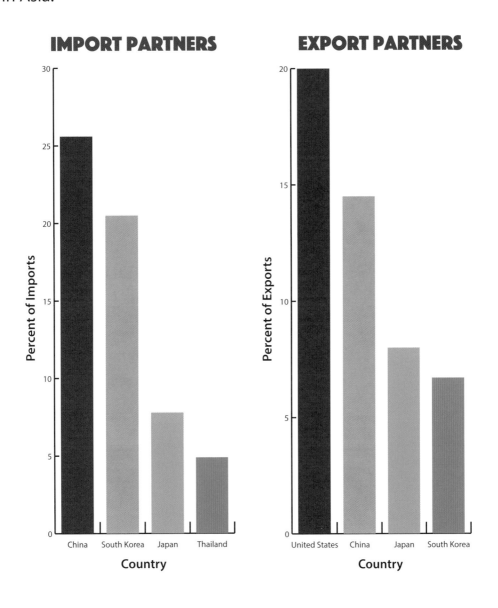

IMPORT PARTNERS

Percent of Imports

Country

China | South Korea | Japan | Thailand

EXPORT PARTNERS

Percent of Exports

Country

United States | China | Japan | South Korea

The United States and Vietnam have a long and complicated history. Both countries are working toward a strong relationship.

Vietnam's government is still completely controlled by the Communist Party. It is the only political party that is allowed to exist. This is stated in the country's most recent **constitution**, from 2013.

ACTIVITY

Percentages show how common something is, based on a total number of 100. (For example, 50 percent means 50 out of 100.) The percentages on the pie chart refer to the employment numbers you read earlier in the chapter. Based on these percentages, which grouping of stick figures represents the number of people involved in agriculture? Which group represents those in industry? Which group represents the number of people who work in services?

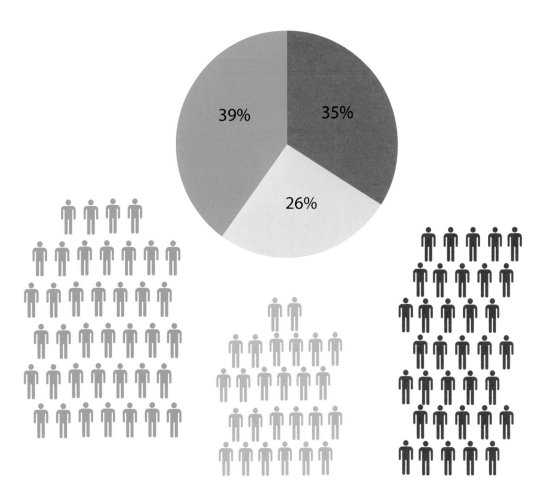

Members of the National Assembly meet in Hanoi. The new National Assembly House opened in 2014.

The National Assembly makes the country's laws and oversees the economy. Its members also elect the president and the prime minister. The president's job is to represent the country. The prime minister is the head of the government. A cabinet of **ministers** works with the prime minister to run the country.

The National Assembly elects the head of the Supreme People's Court. This court helps make sure people and the government uphold the laws.

Vietnam has more than 59 provinces and 5 municipalities, each with its own smaller government. Citizens elect leaders to a local People's Council, which makes laws for that area. That group then elects members to be on a People's Committee to represent the region. The National Assembly still has a lot of control at this level. It can determine which candidates are allowed to run for office.

Flag

Vietnam's flag shows a five-pointed yellow star on a red background. The yellow symbolizes the Vietnamese people. Each point stands for a different group: scholars, farmers, workers, businesspeople, and military personnel. The red on the flag represents blood and revolution.

The People's Committee Building in Ho Chi Minh City was built in 1898. The city's government still meets there today.

CHAPTER 3

MEET THE PEOPLE

Vietnam's first societies sprung up around the Red River about 5,000 years ago. The nation's history is full of battles and disputes about who would control the land. Japan, China, and France all had control at some point. Eventually, Vietnam became an independent country under communist rule. Today, around 97 million people call Vietnam home.

Dragon fruit is a member of the cactus family. This sweet fruit is grown across southern Vietnam.

Stilt houses have been used in Vietnam for around 4,000 years. The design protects them from flood waters. They are also useful in mountainous areas.

Ho Chi Minh City, originally Saigon, was renamed after one of the country's rulers in 1975. Today, it is the largest city, with a population of around 8.4 million. It is full of French architecture from the 19th century. Hanoi, the capital, is the second-largest city, with around 7.4 million people.

More than 60 percent of the population live in the countryside, mostly near the major river deltas. Some houses are built on stilts in case the river floods. Others float directly on the river.

Vietnam is home to 54 different ethnic groups. The Viet people, or Kinh, make up 87 percent of the population. There are around 1 million Hmong people living mostly in the north.

Groups of Hmong people live in southern China, Laos, Thailand, and Vietnam. There are also around 260,000 Hmong people in the United States.

Vietnamese is the country's official language. It is a tonal language. This means that one word can have many different meanings depending on how it is spoken. Tone is the way voices rise or fall. A word can be spelled one way but have up to six different meanings.

English is becoming increasingly popular as a second language that is learned in schools. Some people still speak French or Chinese.

Children are required to go to school for 5 years, usually from ages 6 to 11. Students can choose to do lower secondary school (high school) from ages 11 to 15. Some then study for another 3 years, especially if they want to go to a university. Most schools hold classes 6 days a week, from Monday to Saturday. Students only attend half days.

About 95 percent of Vietnamese children enroll in school. This has resulted in a 90 percent literacy rate in the country.

DRAGON MASK ACTIVITY

During New Year parades, people in costumes form long dragons. They dance down the street to celebrate. These mythical creatures represent luck, power, and intelligence. Make your own dragon mask and have a parade with your friends!

MATERIALS:

- Small cardboard box that fits over head
- Scissors
- Staples or glue
- Construction paper
- Markers or crayons
- Streamers

INSTRUCTIONS:

1. Have an adult help you cut holes in the cardboard box for your eyes and nose.
2. Decorate the box with markers or crayons. Add teeth or horns, plus any other details you can think of.
3. Attach streamers to the back of the box to represent the body and tail. Use glue or a stapler to attach them to the box.
4. Show off your design in a parade!

The dragon dance is performed during New Year parades.

Dragons have been an important symbol in Vietnamese culture for almost 1,000 years.

Placing floating candles in a river is thought to bring good luck.

Vietnam does not have an official religion, but people worship in different ways. Around 45 percent of the population practices a folk or regional religion. Families worship their **ancestors**. They take offerings of flowers, food, and **incense** to family altars or public **pagodas**. People believe their ancestors protect them.

Many people practice a combination of beliefs. They may perform some Buddhist rituals. At the same time, they may also follow the teachings of Confucianism and Taoism. This practice is called *Tam Giáo*, or "Three Religions."

Colonists from Spain, Portugal, and France brought Catholicism to the country. Today, this is practiced by 7 percent of the population. Around 1.5 percent of the country is Protestant. *Hòa Hảo* and *Cao Đài* are religions practiced only in rural parts of Vietnam and neighboring Cambodia.

Incense is burned in temples for many reasons, such as celebrating a new baby.

CHAPTER 4

CELEBRATIONS

Many holidays in Vietnam are cultural or religious. Some celebrate the country's communist state. Families get together for big meals and to watch parades and fireworks.

Tết Nguyên Đán, or Vietnamese New Year, is the most important holiday of the year. It is celebrated in January or February. The date changes every year because it follows the lunar calendar. Each year in the lunar calendar is represented by a different animal from the Chinese zodiac. The year 2021 is the Year of the Ox.

Colorful paper lanterns are used to decorate the streets during New Year celebrations.

Many people believe that kitchen gods protect their families. These are three gods who watch over the household. They bring luck and happiness to families. The week before *Tết*, families hold a big feast to thank them. Honoring ancestors is another important part of this time of year. Some people visit cemeteries to invite their dead relatives to the festivities.

People pray for good luck during *Tết*. Several customs bring good luck. One is inviting a successful visitor over to the house. Children are given lucky money called *lì xì* in red envelopes.

HOLIDAYS AND CELEBRATIONS

January 1 – **New Year's Day**

January or February – ***Tết Nguyên Đán*** (Vietnamese New Year)

February or March – **Lantern Festival**

April (date changes) – **Hùng Kings' Temple Festival**

April 30 – **Reunification Day**

June 1 – **International Children's Day**

September 2 – **National Day** (Independence from France)

September or October – ***Trung Thu*** (Mid-Autumn Festival)

December 25 – **Christmas**

LANTERN ACTIVITY

For *Trung Thu*, children parade in the streets with lanterns. Make your own lantern to celebrate!

MATERIALS:

- Pencil
- 2 pieces of vellum paper, a stiff paper found at craft stores
- Scissors
- Hole puncher
- Yarn
- Glow stick or small flashlight
- Wooden dowel

INSTRUCTIONS:

1. With a pencil, draw a star shape on a piece of vellum paper. Cut it out with scissors.

2. Trace this star onto the other piece of paper and cut it out. Now you have two stars of the same size. Fold each star in half along one of the points and then unfold. Then fold it in half again at each point, for a total of five times. (Your stars will have 10 lines coming out from the center.)

3. Place the two stars together so they are perfectly lined up. Punch evenly spaced holes around the edges.

4. Separate the stars, and refold the creases so that the longer creases (the ones at each point) fold out, like a mountain, and the shorter creases fold in like a valley. Your stars will be three-dimensional.

5. Place the stars together again, lined up at the holes. Thread yarn through the hole at the top of one point, going through both stars. Leave a tail about 12 inches (30 cm) long. Sew the yarn over and under through the holes around the outside of the stars.

6. Before you get back to the top, tie a glow stick or small flashlight to the yarn and let it hang down into the star. Finish sewing up to the top point.

7. Tie the two ends of the yarn together to keep it secure. Then tie the ends to a wooden dowel. Now you have a lantern!

Offerings such as fruit are placed on altars in temples and in people's homes.

Mooncakes are only eaten around the time of Trung Thu. *People enjoy them with a cup of black or green tea.*

Trung Thu is another important celebration. The Mid-Autumn Festival honors children and is held in September or October. Children listen to stories and eat mooncakes. These treats can be sweet or savory. Most are round, but some come in different shapes like rabbits or lanterns. During this festival, children wear masks that look like lions. They bang on drums or carry lanterns and parade through the streets. It is also a time to give thanks.

In Vietnam, two calendar systems are used. The lunar calendar, based on the cycles of the moon, is used to determine when holidays will fall. The Western calendar is used for daily life and activities.

LUNAR CALENDAR	WESTERN CALENDAR
12 months	12 months
29–30 days in a month	28–31 days in a month
One year = 354 days	One year = 365 days
Every 3rd year, a month is added to better match the Western calendar.	Every 4th year, an extra day is added.

The city of Da Lat in the Central Highlands is known for its natural beauty and French architecture.

Many children play soccer after school. Some play on teams at soccer clubs. Others play with friends.

People play many different sports and games in Vietnam. Soccer is the most popular. Gymnastics and net sports, such as table tennis and badminton, are also enjoyed. *Sepak takraw* is similar to volleyball, although players use their feet to lob a ball over the net. Vietnam has a long history of martial arts. There are many different styles depending on the region. One is a form of wrestling called *Đấu Vật*. Wrestlers compete during New Year celebrations.

Soccer

Soccer is such a popular sport in Vietnam that people will celebrate losses, as well as wins. As long as their team makes a goal, they're happy! Sometimes there have been riots or violence in the streets after soccer matches. When Vietnam was split into North and South Vietnam, there were two national teams. Northern Vietnam was only allowed to play teams from other communist countries.

CHAPTER 5

WHAT'S FOR DINNER?

Rice is Vietnam's main crop. It can show up at breakfast, lunch, or dinner as a side dish. Many snacks also involve rice. This staple food even shows up in certain desserts, like pudding. Rice is used to make many other products, such as vinegar or noodles.

Pho is a popular soup made with rice noodles. It is often considered Vietnam's national dish. The recipe was created in northern Vietnam in the 1880s. The dish mixes traditional Vietnamese flavors with Chinese spices. Although the dish is sometimes served with chicken, it was traditionally made with beef. This is an influence from French cuisine.

Pho was first eaten in the northern mountain ranges where temperatures are colder. Now, the dish is popular throughout the country.

Night markets offer many different dinner choices.

Fresh ingredients are important in Vietnamese cuisine. Food is often cooked in water or broth instead of oil. This makes it healthier. It also helps keep the taste fresh and light. Herbs and spices such as cilantro, mint, lemongrass, and ginger add to the flavor. Red chili makes dishes spicy.

Crab, prawn, shrimp, and fish are all found along the country's coastline. People also eat poultry, pork, and beef. Other meats would be considered unusual in the United States, such as snake, frog, and bat.

Snacks in Vietnam Markets

Markets floating in the water or crowded along city streets sell everything from fish and meat to vegetables and fruits. Street vendors set up stalls and make pho, spring rolls, or sweet snacks. Some walk around with food and utensils in baskets. They make fresh meals right on the spot.

Fresh food is an important part of Vietnamese cuisine. Many people shop at local markets.

Different fruits grow well in the nation's tropical climate. Bananas, coconuts, **durians**, **rambutans**, and **pomelos** are sold in local markets. Vegetables are common side dishes at homes and in restaurants. They can be served raw or pickled.

Fish sauce called *nước mắm* is an important condiment. Salt and fish are layered in barrels for up to a year to make this sauce. People add it to their food at the table.

Popular drinks include tea, coffee, fruit juice, coconut milk, and soft drinks. These often come from local products.

RECIPE

Families enjoy making large batches of fresh spring rolls to share. Rice paper is filled with vegetables and thin noodles, then rolled. The rolls are served fresh and not fried. Sometimes they are called summer rolls, since they are a refreshing snack during the hot and humid summer months.

INGREDIENTS:

SPRING ROLLS

- 2 ounces (57 grams) of rice vermicelli (noodles)
- 8 rice wrappers
- 1 tablespoon (1.6 grams) of chopped Thai basil
- 3 tbsp (4.8 g) of chopped mint leaves
- 3 tbsp (4.8 g) of chopped cilantro
- 2 leaves of lettuce, chopped
- 1 carrot, cut into long, thin strips (additional vegetables like red pepper or cucumber can also be used)
- Optional: fried tofu, shredded chicken, or shrimp

DIPPING SAUCE

- ¼ cup (59 milliliters) of water
- 2 tbsp (30 ml) of fresh lime juice
- 1 clove of garlic, cut into small pieces
- 2 tbsp (25 g) of white sugar
- ½ teaspoon (2.5 ml) of garlic chili sauce
- 3 tbsp (45 ml) of fish sauce

INSTRUCTIONS:

1. Fill a medium saucepan with water and bring it to a boil. Cook the rice vermicelli 3 to 5 minutes, then drain.

2. Fill a large bowl with warm water. Dip one rice wrapper into the water for 1 second to make it soft. Lay the wrapper flat. In a row across the center, add vermicelli, herbs, lettuce, vegetables, and optional meat or tofu. Leave about 2 inches (5 cm) uncovered on each side so the wrap won't be overfilled.

3. Fold uncovered sides inward, then tightly roll the wrapper. Repeat with remaining ingredients.

4. Mix the ingredients for the dipping sauce together in a small bowl.

5. Serve spring rolls with fish sauce mixture.

Many different spices and herbs are used in Vietnamese dishes.

Flavors

Many Vietnamese cooks try to balance five flavor elements in their dishes. They often try to get each flavor into every dish. Some people believe these flavors represent five elements of the earth. Sweet flavors represent the earth. Sour tastes are connected to wood. Saltiness reminds people of water. Bitter notes stand for fire. Spicy tastes represent metal.

Banh mi is a French-Vietnamese sandwich that was created in the late 1800s. During that time, Vietnam was a French colony. The sandwich is served on traditional French bread called a baguette. It is filled with meat, pickled vegetables, and cilantro.

There are many Chinese restaurants in cities. Instead of Chinese soy sauce, many dishes there are prepared with fish sauce. This makes the flavor more traditionally Vietnamese. Architecture, festivals, and food all celebrate Vietnam's rich history and culture.

Banh mi sandwiches are available on many street corners. Workers eat them as a quick meal for breakfast or lunch.

GLOSSARY

ancestors *(AN-sess-turz)* people from whom one is descended

communist *(KOM-yuh-nist)* having to do with a type of government with an economy that is based on public or state control of property and business

constitution *(kon-sti-TOO-shun)* a document that sets up a government system

delta *(DEL-tuh)* an area of land made by deposits of mud or sand where a river spreads out or overflows

durians *(DUR-ee-unz)* large, oval fruits with prickly rinds

exporter *(EK-spor-ter)* a country that sends a product to another country to be sold there

incense *(IN-sens)* a stick that lets off a pleasing smell when burned

ministers *(MIN-ih-sturz)* the heads of certain departments in a government

monsoon *(mahn-SOON)* seasonal wind that brings rain

pagodas *(puh-GOH-duhs)* buildings with curved roofs used as places of worship or reflection

pomelos *(POM-uh-loz)* large yellow or orange citrus fruits

rambutans *(ram-BOO-tenz)* bright red, spiny fruits

textile *(TEK-styl)* fabric made by knitting or weaving

typhoon *(tye-FOON)* swirling storm that forms over tropical waters

FOR MORE INFORMATION

BOOKS

O'Connor, Jim. *What Was the Vietnam War?* New York, NY: Penguin Workshop, 2019.

Stuck in Vietnam: Culture Book for Kids. Newark, DE: Speedy Publishing LLC, 2017.

WEBSITES

Embassy of the Socialist Republic of Vietnam
http://vietnamembassy-usa.org/vietnam
This official site of the Embassy of Vietnam is filled with facts about the people, government, economy, and culture of the country.

Kids World Travel Guide: Vietnam Facts for Kids
https://www.kids-world-travel-guide.com/vietnam-facts.html
Visit countries around the world with these sightseeing guides. The page on Vietnam offers a tour of its places and people.

National Geographic Kids: Vietnam
http://kids.nationalgeographic.com/kids/places/find/vietnam
Find facts, photos, videos, and maps of Vietnam at this site.

INDEX

ABOUT THE AUTHOR

Meghan Gottschall is a writer and former university lecturer in French. She loves to travel to new places, but has to admit it's been a while. Meghan currently lives in the Midwest with her husband and two young sons.